Lake Como
Travel Guide

Sightseeing, Hotel, Restaurant
& Shopping Highlights

Thomas Kirby

Table of Contents

Lake Como

Located in the Lombardy region in northern Italy, Lake Como is one of the most picturesque tourist destinations in Italy. The beauty of the lake and its surrounding areas has made it a favorite vacation spot for the rich and famous. The beauty of Lake Como has featured in many novels, stories, movies, and music videos. The stunning Alps, grand lakeside villas, medieval churches and the serenity of nature make it a tourist magnet attracting visitors year round.

Lake Como is shaped like an inverted alphabet 'Y'. Spanning 146 sq km, and running 400 ft deep, it is the 3rd largest lake in Italy and one of the deepest in Europe. The region surrounding the lake in the southern parts are quite flat but make way to the Alpine foothills in the north.

Along the shore are many beautiful small towns and villages. Towns like Como, Bellagio, Varenna, and Menaggio are not only picture perfect, they also have a very relaxed and laid back atmosphere. Such tranquility and beauty have attracted many celebrities to Lake Como over the years. Lake Como has featured as a private vacation home for celebrities like Sylvester Stallone, Madonna, and Versace. One of the most famous people resident here in recent years is George Clooney. His lakeside villa in the town of Laglio has drawn much public and media attention especially after his marriage there in 2014. In fact, the local government is reputed to slap a fine on any boat coming within 100 yards of it! But do not be surprised to bump on to Clooney in a quiet bar as he often heads in to town without much fanfare.

It is not only Clooney who has been hooked by the beauty of Lake Como. The aristocratic villas bear testimony to the popularity of the region to the rich and the famous for centuries. In fact its natural beauty has been appreciated from as old as the Roman times! Today, Lake Como not only is a haven for nature lovers, the architecture and the myriad cultural activities keeps visitors of all ages and interest equally involved.

Culture

There are a number of festivals and events in the culture calendar of Lake Como. Operas, theaters, street markets, traditional festivals, and a variety of celebrations keep everyone entertained.

One of the newer but very popular festivals is the Lake Como Festival. Organized since 2006, this bilingual – Italian and English – classical music festival attracts many domestic and international artists. With the backdrop of the Alpine mountains and the beautiful villas, it is an experience of one of its kind. The Schignano Carnival is an annual traditional carnival where many medieval events are reenacted. The Baredello Festival in Como and the Pesa Vegia in Bellano are also medieval costume carnivals that liven up the towns every year. Other popular traditional festivals include the Premana Rivive and the feast of Sagre delle Sagre. Every year the picturesque lakeshore towns are decked up with many Christmas markets where one can buy many traditional crafts and food items.

Theater lovers would be spoilt for choice in the Lake Como region. Not only are there a number of theaters, many of these were built over a century ago and are regarded as attractions themselves for their architectural beauty. Leading the pack is the historic 19th century Teatro Sociale. Other theaters in the lake region include the Teatro Della Societa and the Teatro Sala Polifunzionale in Lecco, the Teatro dei Burattini de Como, and the Griante in Municipio. Families with kids can head to the Fata Morgana Theater which has been rolling out productions for children.

In spite of its relaxed atmosphere, there is a very vibrant night scene in Lake Como. There are numerous clubs, discos, and bars where one have a drink or dance until dawn! Popular clubs include the Passion Club with its large dance floor and theme nights. The Orsa Maggiore Disco plays Latin music and is also equipped with a restaurant and a lido! Club 29 and Lido di Lenno also draw large crowds, especially on weekends.

There are many options for food lovers in Como. Other than the festivals and traditional events where one can try traditional food and wine, there are many restaurants and cafes in almost every town. Fish items dominate many restaurant menus but if one is strictly looking for a traditional food item then it has be polenta – a cornmeal porridge served with meat or cheese. Risotto – Persian fish made with onion, butter, and white wine is also worth trying.

Location & Orientation

Lake Como is located in northern Italy very close to the Switzerland border. In fact, the Swiss border is less than 5 km from the town of Como. Milan is the closest major city to Como; at a distance of about 37 km. Other major Italian cities like Genoa, Verona, and Turin are all within a distance of 150 km from the Lake Como region.

The nearest major airport to Lake Como is the Milano-Malpensa Airport - http://www.milanomalpensa-airport.com/en, IATA: MXP. This airport in Milan is about 56 km from Como and has international connections to many cities including Moscow, Shanghai, Dubai, New York City, Berlin, Barcelona, Miami, Toronto, Istanbul, and London, to name just a few. From the airport the best way to get to Como is to take the Malpensa Express towards Milan, and then change to a train to Como from the Saronno Station. The whole journey (less than €10) should take less than 90 minutes. There are also a number of private coaches and taxis at the airport but those would be comparatively more expensive. Visitors can also arrive at the Linate Airport in Milan - http://www.milanolinate-airport.com/en, IATA: LIN. Although it has lesser flights than Malpensa, the airport is closer to the city of Milan than the Malpensa. Another even smaller airport serving the region is the Bergamo Orio al Serio Airport - http://www.sacbo.it/Airpor/portalProcess.jsp, IATA: BGY which is about 45 km from the city of Milan. From this airport one can take the shuttle to the Bergamo station which has hourly train connections with Lecco.

Trenitalia and LeNORD run many train connections from Como and Lecco to various Italian cities in the Lombardy lines (Line R). Other than to cities like Milan and Bergamo, one can also get international connections to cities like Amsterdam, Frankfurt, Dusseldorf, and Basel. Travelling by train to other cities in the Lombardy region is inexpensive and comfortable. A one-way ticket from Milan costs less than €4.

Travelling by road to Lake Como can be a very enjoyable experience because of the scenic beauty. Most of the connections are through Milan. The E35 motorway connects Milan to Lake Como and then goes further past in to Switzerland. There are many bus services to Lake Como. Other than the airport-express services, there is the popular Eurolines and a few private tour operators like Travel 55 and Travelsphere. Road travel is also popular from Bergamo and Lugano (Switzerland).

Once in the Lake Como region, one can use various means of transport to move around. While the town centers are easily covered by foot, one can use the bus or the train to move from one town to another. The western shore is better connected by bus whereas the eastern shore has more train connections. There are many boat and hydrofoil services for those who want to take the water route. Driving is an option, but the narrow winding roads can be a challenge, especially during the tourist season. Motorcycles are a better option. Fitness enthusiasts can also hire bicycles as there are many rental stores all along Lake Como.

Climate & When to Visit

The Lake Como region has a Mediterranean-like humid subtropical climate. Summer months (May to Sep) have an average high of about 28 degrees Celsius and an average low of about 19 degrees. The winter months (Nov to March) are cold and chilly.

Average temperatures during these months rise to around 7 or 8 degree Celsius with lowest falling just below freezing. Summer months are prone to quick and heavy showers – the wettest being May. Although Lake Como attracts tourists all the year round, the most pleasant weather is just around pre-summer and post-summer seasons.

Sightseeing Highlights

Como

The town of Como is located on the southern tip on the western branch of Lake Como. The city is known for its beautiful medieval architecture and picturesque lakefront, but mostly for its location – on one end Como has excellent connections with Milan and Bergamo, on the other, it is a gateway to the rest of the Como region. Although Como is the 3rd most visited place in Lombardy – after Milan and Bergamo - it has often been used just as a stopover destination before visiting the more picturesque and touristy destinations on Lake Como.

However, Como has enough attractions worthy of making it more than a stopover town. Churches, museums, medieval architecture, along with an abundance of outdoor activities and a vibrant nightlife make Como an enjoyable destination for visitors of all interest.

Como is well connected by train and bus from the airports in Milan and Bergamo. Regular train connections are also available with many other countries in Europe. The E35 motorway connects the town with Milan at one direction and the very popular tourist resort of Lugano (Switzerland) on the opposite direction. Within Como one can use the Autolinee bus service or the taxi to move around although, most of the town can be covered by foot. Bicycle rentals are available at http://www.bikeonly.it/. There are over half a dozen parking garages in town for those who are driving in.

Outdoor Activities

One of the first things to do in Como is to take a walk on the waterfront. Boat rides are available for those who want to visit the neighboring lakeshore towns. One can also bike to the nearby border of Switzerland by riding across the hill at Como. Horseback riding and hiking are also options in the outskirts of Como. The beaches in Como offer a relaxed atmosphere. There are also a number of lidos for those who are looking for some fun and amusements.

Funicular Railway

The funicular ride is a great way to enjoy the natural beauty of Como as well as have a glance of rural Como. Established in 1894 and modernized in 1911, the funicular proudly maintains all safety features of the modern day in spite of its age. The funicular ride connects Como with Brunate. During the ride one can have stunning views of the lake and the surrounding mountains. At the top, other than the panoramic views, one can enjoy the Pissarottino Fountain. One can also climb further up to the Volta Lighthouse at the peak. On the way down one can simply walk by the tracks or take a number of different routes. There is also a shuttle service to take people downhill. The funicular operates from 6 am until 10:30 am every day except Saturdays when it operates until midnight.

Como Cathedral

Built in 1740, the Como Cathedral is often regarded as the last cathedral in Italy built in a Gothic style. It replaced a Romanesque cathedral on the same site, construction of which had started in the late 14th century. This dominating structure can be identified by its 75 m high dome. It stretches 87 m in length and is 56 m at its widest. The floor plan of the cathedral resembles a Latin Cross. Inside there is a central nave and 2 aisles with a Renaissance transept. The interior is beautifully decorated with a 16th century choir. The tapestries from the 17th century came from Antwerp, Florence, and Ferrara. The 'modern' touch is provided by colorful stained glass windows that were added in the 19th century.

Teatro Sociale

The Teatro Sociale was built in 1813 to replace the outdated 18th century theater in town. The new theater was built with membership subscriptions. It replaced the ruins of Torre Rotondo, a medieval castle. Construction started with the neo-classical façade that was planned well in advance. However, by 1854, the theater had to be expanded. Yearlong expansions added 38 new boxes to take the total up to 98. It was again expanded in 1910 when another house was added. The present structure is from the remodeling of 1984. It now has a seating capacity of 900 separated into 5 tiers.

The interior of the theater is adorned with a cello-shaped auditorium, red-velvet seats, sculpted walls, and a number of priceless paintings. The theater hosts many performances throughout the year, ranging from children's plays to operas. Even if one is not planning to watch a performance, it is worth the time to visit the Teatro Sociale just to admire the building.

Volta Temple

The Volta Temple – Tempio Voltiano to the locals – is a museum housed in a beautiful neoclassical building and dedicated to the scientist and inventor Alessandro Volta. Volta, who lived his last years in Como is credited to having invented the electrical battery.

The museum and the portrait of Volta used to feature in the 10000 lira banknote of Italy before the currency was replaced by the Euro. The Volta Temple is one of the most visited museums in Lake Como. It displays many scientific instruments and personal belongings of the scientist.

Attractions in Como are not limited to the ones listed above. Other attractions in town include the Civic Archeological Museum and the History Museum. There is also a war memorial at the waterfront. A walk in the walled old town will also take one past many historic buildings that have stood the passage of time. 2 walks are specially recommended – the 'Romantic Promenade Walk' along the western shore of the lake and the Night Walk from Torre Civica to the Piazza Cavour via the Cathedral Square.

Bellagio

The picture postcard town of Bellagio is situated at the junction of the 3 branches of Lake Como. This beautiful lakeshore town along with its incredibly stunning natural surroundings makes it a must-visit place when in Lake Como. Its strategic location at the peninsula coupled with its beauty earned it the nickname – Pearl of Lake Como.

Bellagio is well connected with Como by train and bus. Within the city one can take a guided tour or simply walk around aimlessly and admire the hamlets and luxurious villas.

Villa Serbelloni

One of the most popular villas in Bellagio is the Villa Serbelloni on via Roma. The original villa was built in 1485 replacing a country house which, in turn, had replaced a castle on the same site. The villa went through major renovations and expansions in the 17th century and was given the grand look that we see today. It has been owned by a number of aristocratic families over the centuries, including Ella Walker, the owner of the popular Canadian Club Whiskey; since 1959 it is under the Rockefeller Foundation. The villa is not open to the public but the surrounding garden is.

The Serbelloni garden which includes the wooded hill behind the town can only be visited through a guided tour. The tour is not only informative; one can also enjoy panoramic views of Bellagio that cannot be seen from any other place. However, one cannot go close to the garden by the villa as it is reserved for the guests of the foundation. The guided tours are available for a minimum of 6 and a maximum of 30 people. There are two 90-minute tours daily at 11:30 am and 3:30 pm. It costs €9 per person with discounts for children and seniors.

Villa Melzi

Built in 1810, the Villa Melzi is a neoclassical gem with a Japanese Garden, a monument to Dante, and Azaleas steps. The Etruscan cinerary on the left of the building entrance dates back to the 3rd century BC. The outside of the villa has a number of Egyptian and Roman sculptural engravings.

The interior, which is not open to the public, has beautiful wooden furnishings, paintings, sculptures, and frescoes.

The beautifully landscaped garden surrounding the villa has Japanese maples, rhododendrons, and American redwoods. Do not miss the statute of the Egyptian goddess Pacht that Napoleon had gifted to one of the former owners of the villa. The English styled garden overlooks the lake bringing a tremendous sense of tranquility. The neatly laid out bushes and shrubs are done in complete harmony with the villa. The garden is open to the public in the summer months from 9:30 am to 6:30 pm.

Other villas in Bellagio include the Villa del Balbianello and the Villa Trotti.

Churches in town

Two churches worth visiting in Bellagio are the Church of Madonna del Rosario and the San Giovanni Church. The former is a church built in a Romanesque style of architecture that has a number of priceless pieces of art adorning its interior. The latter is decorated with a number of beautiful sculptures. A short walk takes one to the ruins of a 10th century monastery nestled in the hilltop caves.

Bellagio has a number of restaurants, cafes, and nightclubs - all aimed at visiting tourists as the population of the town is very low. One of the highlights in town is the open air opera. With the backdrop of the lake and the alpine peaks, the operas are almost a surreal experience.

Menaggio

Located about halfway along the western shore of Lake Como is the town of Menaggio. Although the town does not have too many attractions, it is an excellent place to enjoy a number of outdoor activities. Menaggio is well connected by bus from not only Como and Bergamo, but also from the Swiss holiday town of Lugano. This once strategic town was fortified with walls and a castle. This hill side can be clearly separated into two distinct sections. The old town on the side of the hill has more medieval architecture and the section near the foot of the hill has a more 'modern' 19th century look. The old town presents narrow alleys, stone buildings, and steep cobbled stairways whereas the newer part of town has luxurious villas, tree-lined promenade, and many al fresco restaurants and cafes.

Once in town, one of the first things to do would be to take a walk along the lake promenade to enjoy the serenity and beauty of Menaggio. A short climb up the hill and one is transported back by a few centuries.

Amongst the religious monuments in town, one can see the Parish church of St Stephen. This Romanesque styled church has a richly decorated chapel that is visually very appealing. The town also has the Baroque styled church of St Charles and the Saviour's Fountain.

One of the highlights of Menaggio is the historic Menaggio and Cadenabbia Golf Club. Founded in 1903, the club not only offers a beautiful green course but also a spectacular backdrop with the lake and the Alpine peaks. The length of this 18 hole course is 5476 m. Visitors can play in this course with a fee (weekdays €55; weekends €70). Clubs and buggies are also available on hire. The town also has a sports center and a lido for those looking for a swim or a tan.

Varenna

Located on the eastern shore of Lake Como, Varenna completes the golden triangle of Lake Como, along with Belaggio and Menaggio. The town is probably the most visited on the eastern shore. The golden triangle is so popular with the tourists that it has its own ferry route and service.

The shaded lakeside promenade of Varenna is similar to that of Menaggio; on the other hand, the narrow cobbled pathways leading to the old town up the hill are similar to that of Bellagio.

The town of Varenna, however, is quieter and less touristy than the other two. Varenna also attracts more Italian visitors due to its direct rail connection with Milan. One of the delights is to try the locally made gelato (ice-cream) that is sold by a number of stalls on the lakeside promenade.

Castello Di Vezio

This is the most visited tourist attraction of Varenna. This 13th century castle is perched on a hilltop and has excellent views of the lake and the town, especially from the olive garden and the top of the viewing tower. The biggest draw of the castle is the close encounter with the birds of prey that are trained and maintained there. With a ticket one can meet the falconer and have a chance to see the birds 'perform' at close range. If lucky, one may even get the chance to hold one of the birds of prey. The falconer is present from 10 am to 6 pm everyday and trains the birds in front of the visitors. Special shows are held almost every day at 2:30 pm. However, the display and the castle are closed in bad weather and in the winter months. There is an entry fee of €4 with discounts for children and seniors.

Villa Monastero

Villa Monsatero is one of the few villas that has been accredited as a museum and is open to the public. Like most other villas, it is on the lakefront and is surrounded by a beautifully laid out garden.

The garden stretches for nearly 2 km and has different sections like the citrus collection, a formal terrace, a grand landing platform, and a promenade adorned with sculptures. There is a narrow pathway separating the garden from the lake which has a number of benches where one can sit and enjoy the spectacular views. The villa which is now rented out for conferences and meetings is worth visiting to see the grandeur of the decorations and the furnishings. It is open daily in the summer months (Mar to Nov) from 9:30 am to 7 pm. There is an entry fee of €8 with discounts for children and seniors.

Tremezzo

The small town of Tremezzo is located on the western shore of Lake Como about 20 km from Como and on the opposite shore of Bellagio. It is connected by bus and ferry services from both Como and Bellagio. For centuries, Tremezzo has been known for its mild climate, beautiful gardens, and luxurious villas.

There is a small public park that leads out to the lake where one can go for a swim in the clear azure water of Lake Como. A relaxed stroll of the town will take one to the 18th century parish church of San Lorenzo.

The town has a number of villas like the La Carlia, Amila, and the Meier which are privately owned. The luxurious Grand Hotel Tremezzo is also housed in a villa. But the one villa that is open to the public and is a major tourist attraction is the Villa Carlotta. Tremezzo also has a lot of lush greenery, primarily because of its location where it is protected from strong cold winds. Historically, it has been popular for its olive gardens and the production of oil.

Villa Carlotta

Sprawling a massive 17 acres, the Villa Carlotta was built in 1690 for the marquis of Milan – Giorgio Clerici. It is named after Charlotte, the Duchess of Saxe-Meiningen, who received the villa as a wedding gift from her mother – Princess Marianna of Prussia. The villa faces the peninsula of Bellagio and is decorated with an Italian garden that is adorned with sculptures and fountains. In fact, the fascinating works of art in the garden and the surrounding park made the villa one of the most famous in the Lake Como region. Rhododendrons, azaleas, camellias, ferns, and even bamboo trees compliment the beauty of the villa garden. The garden also has a museum of agricultural tools. The 2 floors of the house museum have a variety of items in display. While the first floor has many works of art from the 18th and 19th centuries, the second floor displays furniture and household items from the days of Charlotte. The villa area also includes a book store, a café, and a couple of picnic spots. The villa and the garden are open in the summer months (Mar to Oct) from 10 am to 6 pm and have an entry fee of €9.

Comacina Island

In the first glance, Comacina Island looks like a green teardrop in the Lake Como. This small lush green island may look uninhabited and deserted but has been the witness to many historical events. The whole island was used as a fortress in the middle ages. Controlled by the Byzantine garrison, the island was in the side of Milan and fought against Como in the '10 year war'. The island was donated to the Italian government by the King of Belgium in 1919.

Attractions on the island include a number of archeological sites with remains from the Roman era. There are also the ruins of 7 Byzantine churches. The island was a favorite of many Italian and Belgian artists and one of the features is the artist's homes. The most popular are the 3 homes built in the late 1930s by Pietro Lingeri – simply named as A, B, and C. These simple stone houses have two floors with a kitchen, bedroom, toilet, and a studio. These houses were built as vacation homes for the visiting artists. The island, spreading hardly 6 hectares, is a nature lover's delight. It is wrapped in lush Mediterranean greenery giving it a warm and soothing atmosphere. There is also a hospital complex and an Antiquarium Museum on the island.

Lake Maggiore

Located about 5 km west of Lake Como is the beautiful tourist resort of Lake Maggiore.

With a length of 63 km and 10 km at its widest, it is the 2nd largest lake in Italy. About a fifth of the northern part of the lake is in Switzerland.

The lake, formed from a glacier, is surrounded by hills in the southern parts, and the taller Alpine mountains along the northern shores. The mild climate, many picturesque lakeshore towns, and a host of outdoor activities make Lake Maggiore a very popular tourist destination.

Lake Maggiore is located 20 km north of the Malpensa Airport. The western shore is well connected by rail with Milan and Geneva. The lakeshore towns like Stresa, Arona, Verbania, and Baveno have regular bus connections.

Attractions of Lake Maggiore include the cable car ride to the Mottarone Mountain peak from Stresa. Other than its panoramic viewpoints, the mountain is popular for hiking in the summer months and for skiing in the winter months. Stresa is also the stop to take the ferry to the picturesque Borromeo Archipelago with its 3 islands – Bella, Madre, and Pescatori. The Santa Ana Gorge on the Cannabino River is a favorite for kayaking and white water rafting. Outdoor enthusiasts will also enjoy mountain biking and hiking in Mercurago near Arona. For the nature lovers there is the Villa Pallavicino Park near Stresa. The park has a botanical garden and a zoo and is open in the summer months only. The picturesque Villa Taranto Botanical Gardens is located in Verbania. Lovers of history and archeology will enjoy the 12th century Santa Caterina del Sasso Church, the Cannero Castle, the Angera Castle, and the Arona Fortress.

It is recommended to carry Swiss Francs along with Euros if travelling along the Lake as many places in the Swiss border do not accept Euros. The whole of Lake Maggiore is a tourist attraction, so, if planning to travel from Lake Como, one should have at least a couple of days to have a feel of the area.

Madesimo Ski Resort

The Madesimo Ski Resort is located about 70 km north of Lake Como and about 110 km from Milan. The resort is near the Swiss border. While the area is popular for hiking in the summer months, it is a popular ski resort in the winter months.

Madesimo is best reached by car. The Via Spluga or SS36 runs from the Lake Como region to Madesimo. One need not drive all the way to the skiing area. There is a free (only on weekdays) parking zone in Campodolcino from where there is a funicular connection to Madesimo. However, it is recommended that good snow tires are used if taking a car to Madesimo in winter. For those who prefer public transport can opt for the bus, train, or taxi share.

Madesimo is more popular with the local Italians and is very busy on the weekends, so it is preferable if one can visit the place on weekdays. It is part of the skiing area of Valchiavenna.

With just over 50 km of trails, it is one of the smaller resorts in northern Italy but offers a host of activities. Golf, biking, camping, indoor football, canoeing, rock climbing, and swimming are popular in Madesimo. The adventurous can also try snow-kite surfing. For those who want to strictly stick to skiing, there are a number of rental stores to get the skiing accessories. Amateurs can also opt for a professional guide.

Recommendations for a Budget Traveller

Places to Stay

Albergo Milano Hotel

Via XX Settembre 35., Varenna
Tel: 39 0341 830 298
http://www.varenna.net/ENG/Servizi.html

Located in the historic center of Varenna.

The Albergo Milano has been welcoming guests since the early 20th century. The hotel is ideal for those who are looking for a romantic getaway and even for those who are looking for a quiet relaxed vacation. It has retained many of its original furnishings and décor thus giving the guest a feeling of the yesteryears. The hotel has a beautiful terrace and an al fresco restaurant. It has free parking and free Wi-Fi.

Rooms have TV, safe, minibar, and fan. Room rates start from €130 and include breakfast.

Hotel Bellavista

Via IV Novembre 21
Menaggio
Tel: 39 0344 32136
http://www.hotel-bellavista.org/

This 3 star hotel is located on the lake front of Menaggio. The pier to catch ferries to Como and Bellagio is hardly 150 m away. Facilities include free Wi-Fi and a free outdoor pool. There is a bar and a restaurant. Guests receive a discount at the nearby golf course.

All rooms are ensuite and some are with a verandah facing the lake. Room rates start from €70 and include breakfast.

NH Pontevecchio

Via A Visconti 84
Lecco
Tel: 39 0341 238000
http://www.nh-hotels.com/nh/en/hotels/italy/lecco---lake-como/nh-pontevecchio.html

Located about a 5 minute walk from the historic center of Lecco, the Pontevecchio is a 4 star hotel near the waterfront area. Facilities include 24 hr reception, elevators, free Wi-Fi, free parking, and doctor on call. There is an onsite restaurant and bar.

The ensuite rooms are non-smoking and come with a TV, air-conditioning, minibar, radio, telephone, laundry service, and safe. Room rates start from €90 and include breakfast.

Hotel Plinius

Via Garibaldi 33
Como
Tel: 39 031 273 067
http://www.hotelplinius.com/

This 3 star hotel is located between the Como town center and the lakefront. The station is 300 m away. Public transport is available nearby. Attractions in the vicinity include the Como Cathedral, major shopping streets, and a number of restaurants.

The newly renovated rooms are modern-styled and equipped with free Wi-Fi and satellite TV. Room rates start from €70 and include breakfast.

Best Western Hotel Continental

Viale Innocenzo XI 15
Como
Tel: 39 031 260 485
http://www.hotelcontinentalcomo.it/en/home-page.aspx

Located about a 5 minute walk from the Como historic town center, the Best Western is a 3 star hotel with all the usual modern amenities. The hotel has car park (surcharge), free Wi-Fi, lift, bar, and a restaurant. Outdoor activities like horseriding, tennis, and fishing are available near the hotel.

The ensuite non-smoking rooms have minibar, TV, AC, safe, and hairdryer. Room rates start from €85 and include breakfast.

Places to Eat

Barchetta

Piazza Cavour 1, Como
Tel: 39 031 3221
http://www.hotelbarchetta.it/en/hotel-como-with-restaurant

The Barchetta is part of the Barchetta Excelsior Hotel and is located right on the lakefront. The restaurant has a simple yet elegant décor. Cuisine served is primarily Italian. Starters, rice, and pasta are priced within €15. Non-vegetarian dishes like grilled fish in vegetables, veal shank in herb, and beef fillet in red wine are priced around €25. One can also try a variety of local wine (around €6).

Antica Darsena

Lungo Lario Trieste 16, Como
Tel: 39 031 23391
http://www.palacehotel.it/en/hotel-restaurant-como

The Antica Darsena is located inside the Palace Hotel. With crystal chandeliers, half moon windows, and a spectacular view of the lake, the Antica Darsena is ideal for a romantic or quiet meal.

It serves local and Mediterranean cuisine. Both vegetarian and non-vegetarian starters are priced around €15. Rice and pasta are also priced the same. Entrees include items like prawns in olive (€22), baked lamb with vegetables (€28), and risotto in melted butter (€25). Desserts include mousse, salads, tiramisu, and fruits.

La Vista

Via XX Settembre 35
Varenna
Tel: 39 0341 830 298
http://www.varenna.net/ENG/Ristorante-LaVista.php

This al fresco restaurant overlooks the lake and has spectacular views during sunset and the nighttime. It is part of the Albergo Milano Hotel. The menu, which changes every year, comprises of Mediterranean and Italian dishes. Guests can choose from set menus – 3-course (€38), or 4-course (€45). Dishes include bell peppers in fresh cheese (€14), fish fillet with pink pepper (€19), and wild boar pasta in cheese (€15). It also serves a variety of wine and champagne.

Albergo Valtellina

Via Bellinzona 265, Como
Tel: 39 31 540 750
http://www.albergovaltellina.com/eng/ristorante.php

Part of the Valtellina Hotel, the Albergo Valtellina Restaurant is a small and cozy restaurant serving Italian cuisine. This is also an ideal place to try some traditional local dishes. The restaurant serves a tourist menu (€11 excluding drinks) where one can try a variety of local dishes. Dishes on the a la carte include dried beef, pasta with porcini mushrooms, polenta, and a variety of wine.

Crott del Meo

Via Campora 2
Perledo
Tel: 39 333 225 1298
http://www.crottdelmeo.it/en/kitchen.html

This cozy restaurant serves traditional dishes typical to the lake region. It has a stone cellar for storing wine, cheese, and salami – the 3 specialties of the restaurant. Homemade specialties also include a unique variety of jams – onion jam, pepper jam, and coffee jam! Cakes and ice-cream are also made in-house. It offers a 6-course meal (€28) where guests can select the dishes.

Places to Shop

Azalea

Salita Serbelloni 31
Bellagio
Tel: 39 031 951 333
http://www.azaleabellagio.com/

One of the most popular products from the Lake Como region is silk. Not only are the silk products of a very good quality, they are also much cheaper than in most major cities like Milan. The Azalea is on the busy Serbelloni Street and sells a variety of pure silk products – ties, scarves, bags, and foulards. It also sells shirts and leather items. The Azalea has a branch at Serbelloni 41.

Adhoc

Lungo Lario Manzoni 42-44
Bellagio
Tel: 39 031 950 073
http://www.adhocbellagio.it/index_eng.html

The Adhoc is the authorized dealer of a number of popular Italian brands like Bridge, Emilio Pucci, Gherardini, and Orciani. This is the ideal place for visitors looking for branded Italian leather and silk products. Items on sale include bags, foulards, scarves, leather accessories, hats, and small gift items like key chains.

Max Mara

Via Vittorio Emanule 87
Como
Tel: 39 031 262 321

Located in Como, this is one of the most popular design houses of Italy. The knowledgeable and helpful staff makes shopping at Max Mara a truly enjoyable experience. From the latest trends to the popular classics, Max Mara has a complete collection of various types of clothes and accessories, and that too, at a very reasonable price.

Decio

Via Lusardi 22
Menaggio
Tel: 39 0344 31195

Located in the town center of Menaggio, this homeware boutique is for those who are looking to take home a piece of Italy. Targeting primarily the interior décor market, the store sells items like glassware, candles, soft furnishings, and tableware. There is also a large collection of bed linen. Visitors can also buy gift items from Decio.

Street Markets - Como

Shopping is incomplete in the Lake Como region without a visit to the street markets. From fresh produce to bargain products, the street markets have it all. These markets are usually located in the popular squares and the town hall area. The popular markets include the Haberdashery Market (Viale Varese), Food Market (via Mentana), and Albate Market (via Facioloa). The Saturday-only Crafts and Antiques Market is at Piazza San Fedele.

Printed in Great Britain
by Amazon